IOANNIS TZIVANAKIS

AF273742

life skills
mastery

ITV

CONTENT

For "My" Real Wonders

I.

The Homo Sapiens

Membership

life mastery: the sufficient, complete or very high ability to (a) fulfill the necessities of life and (b) realize as many of life's inherent possibilities as is feasible and appropriate.

In the midst of an overwhelmingly vast ocean of space and matter, we find ourselves on a captivating planet. It is the nourishing shelter of our temporary existence.

The forces and laws of our cosmos as well as the material and ecological conditions of our earthly world belong to the given components of our reality. And they determine our life.

Inside this given and predetermined reality, however, we have different possibilities at our disposal.

If we succeed in using and employing these possibilities effectively, we achieve life mastery.

Within the orderedness or systematics of all living organisms, we humans belong - according to the biological sciences - to the species of Homo sapiens, the rational and wise human being.

Both qualities, reason and wisdom, are given to us by nature and from birth. Thus we are already reasonable and wise at the beginning of our life.

Well then. If we compare ourselves with other species, then that is what we are: reasonable and wise. In certain respects, anyway, or according to certain criteria. Whether this means a finer or multidimensional feeling ability or a multifaceted managing and changing of the given reality.

But when it comes to what is demanded from us in order to fulfill the necessities of life, and to realize as much as possible and appropriate of what is valuable in life, then neither reason nor wisdom are sufficiently present from birth, but must first develop through experience and understanding and thereby also reach an appropriate and possibly decisively effective maturity.

Indeed. Until we are adults, the properties, abilities and qualities of reason and wisdom are not yet sufficiently part of the totality of our abilities.

reason: the ability of logical thinking, understanding and judging.

wisdom: deeper to most profound knowledge acquired through experience and understanding.

And therefore, as long as we are not adults, we depend on the adults responsible for us to enable us to live a life in which both reason and wisdom, as well as all the other fundamental and essentially important life skills, can be experienced, learned, and internalized.

Just what would these life skills be? Or: which ones are they really? And both in our personal larger freedom and in being with others?

What skills are necessary, appropriate, and valuable for life?

What is required for adulthood?

By what is the qualification of adulthood achieved and by what is it decided or established?

II.

The Craft Of

Adulthood

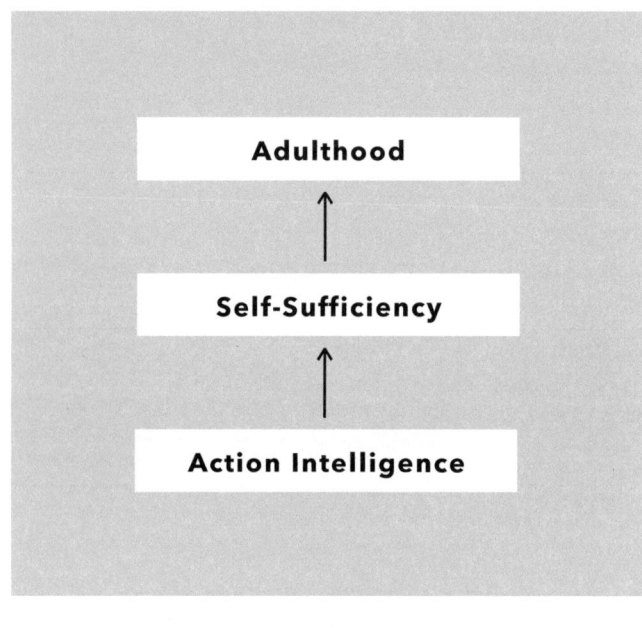

What are we dealing with in life for which adulthood must and should be trained and dynamized?

No question, we consist of energy, so we need energy supply for the continuity of our existence and for all processes of becoming and growing connected with it.

Providing this energy supply in an independent and autonomous way is therefore one of the most basic abilities or even the most basic ability in life.

Because without the necessary energy we lack the power to act. And the more intelligent then this acting becomes and is, the more fruitful are also its results.

Therefore, we can already emphasize here that intelligence of action and self-sufficiency – that is, the knowledge and ability that we need to act sufficiently, appropriately and intelligently and to be self-sufficient both in acting and in general, so that what is necessary for life is ensured – are the primarily most important life skills, and therefore also the qualifying core of adulthood.

Action intelligence basically means concrete and precise doing and does not necessarily (or at least not explicitly) always include behavior.

Everything we do and do not do, together with the way we do something, and the way we are, all this together makes up our behavior.

As a result, our behavior towards others, the way we are and act, is determined when we are with others and not alone.

In an extended and not unimportant form our behavior also has a meaning towards other living beings than only humans as well as towards the whole living nature and earth ecology.

To know, therefore, in what our entire behavior in all these dimensions consists or should reasonably consist, is one of the further central life abilities, because by our behavior we influence and change our fellow world.

However, the prerequisites for the development and internalization of behavioral and action intelligence as well as the necessary self-sufficiency for a stable and contented life are further essential life skills:

We need a general intelligence. That is, the knowledge and ability to see through and understand things and the contents of the world and our lives, as well as to find out and learn what is important and new.

adult: a fully grown person, self-sufficient in life and responsible for his or her own actions.

self-sufficiency: being independent from others (1) in the way to live and to exist and (2) in causing all the necessary resources for the life.

action: psychophysical and usually purposeful application of organismic forces.

intelligence: naturally available or retrievable stored knowledge coupled with the ability to see through, understand, figure out, learn, know something new for oneself and in its possible relationships to others.

behavioral intelligence: the knowledge and ability of appropriate being and acting in being with others.

language intelligence: the mastery of appropriate words and forms of expression to describe content of perceiving, feeling, experiencing, thinking and knowing.

In the same way, we need language intelligence for ourselves and for the areas in our lives that benefit from language, as well as for communication with others.

Very helpful in all this progression through life is the fact that we are also a learning organism by virtue of our "homo sapiens membership".

The ability to learn is innate to us. However, cultivating, deepening and expanding this ability so that we can more successfully master life means enhancing our learning intelligence.

Furthermore, it is not only useful to be rational, since we should and must acknowledge, respect and, yes, affirm the causes and effects within the human condition and the whole of reality, but it is often equally important to be pragmatic, so as not to fail due to inexpedient or muddled and hopeless rigidities.

Such a useful mixture of rationality and pragmatism we achieve and master all the more easily, the more grounded and imbued with realism we are.

All these life skills are part of the craft of adulthood by which we (1) master life with its necessities, and (2) increase this life mastery the more fully we achieve contentment and freedom.

learning intelligence: the masterful knowledge of how learning works.

rationality: the property or ability of inferential reasoning.

realism: the ability or/and way to perceive things as they really are, without becoming or/and being influenced by beliefs, wishful thinking, uncertainty and hope.

pragmatism: the ability or/and way to orient and adapt to real situations and to the knowledge of how these can lead to success when there are problems to solve or goals to achieve.

groundedness: rootedness in the intelligence of the laws of reality and thus of the laws of life as well.

communicational intelligence: the experiential knowledge and the ability, based on it, to communicate appropriately and effectively and to deal with what is communicated.

"Does freedom mean only the absence of external pressure, or does freedom also mean the *presence* of something - and if so, of what?"

Erich Fromm

III.

Contentment
And Freedom

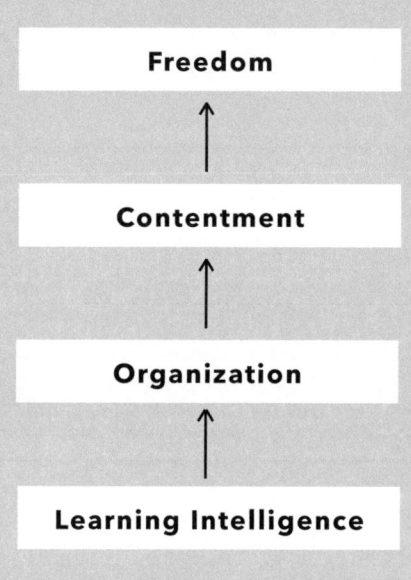

Life is a perpetual cycle of fulfilling necessities and satisfying needs.

We successfully master life when we become self-sufficient in fulfilling both the necessities of life and those needs that enable an enhanced and more nourishing experience of life.

Once our needs are initially tangibly clear, it is only a matter of applying and executing appropriate fulfillment strategies by acting, that is, doing what needs to be done. And we do this through realism and pragmatism. Grounded and rational. And with the appropriate behavior in being with others.

All this together is multifaceted, multi-layered, and for all those who are not prepared for it, very likely overwhelming and possibly unattainable. But for all those who are endowed with the most valuable and important life skills, it all reveals itself as the majestic panorama of the richness of life.

Of a life that may not always smile upon us, but which also always offers an inconceivably huge and, moreover, tappable potential, which under the appropriate circumstances can be transformed into an enhanced life reality.

If we master life by appropriately fulfilling the necessities that life itself imposes upon us, and if we increase our mastery of life the more fully we attain the state of contentment and freedom, and if we become the more satisfied in life the more purposefully and qualitatively we fulfill those needs that enable an increased and more nourishing experience of life, then we must organize our lives in such a way that all our basic needs are satisfied and fulfilled, as well as those needs that deepen and increase the quality of life.

Therefore, organizational intelligence is also one of the most important life skills.

And apart from what intelligent organizing consists of, we organize more effectively and more accurately when we unerringly and deeply understand that we are primarily emotional beings.

Only in coherent and harmonious emotionality can something succeed and also make a substantial contribution to life.

That is why emotional intelligence is one of the most primary life skills. Emotionality must always be

motivational intelligence: (a) the experiential knowledge of one's needs and (b) the sense of real life necessities coupled with (c) the ability to fulfill both.

attention intelligence: the experiential knowledge of the causes of movement and of the nourishing sources of one's attention.

relaxational intelligence: the experiential knowledge of the different dimensions and the corresponding fulfillment processes of (a) one's nourishment and (b) the real necessities of life.

taken into account by all participants and in all matters. It is as much the engine and enabler of action as the basic energy we get from physical nourishment.

Motivational intelligence is just as paramount. What moves us because we are human beings? And what moves us because we are a unique and distinct living being? How do we find out?

Our instrumental ability, given and innate by our human nature, of sensing our motivationality is the function and also task of our attention.

Our attention shows us automatically, self-luminously-knowingly, what we need and therefore want. However, it shows it accurately when we can be as we have been thought to be as a unique living being. By means of the laws of reality as a whole and additionally and especially by means of the biological-psychological laws of the human reality.

Attention intelligence therefore and also authenticity are as life skills the guarantees for the fact that our life is rooted in the reality and feeds and nourishes fulfillingly itself from the fertile soil of this reality and as a result blossoms and vibrates contentedly.

authenticity: the way of being that results from the respective sensed reality of all that expresses itself naturally and unhindered as our entire organismicity: as the "universe" of the energy flow of the perpetual cycle of being-sensing-needing-getting-becoming-being...

feel: to be touched or filled by the senses or by an inner energy.

freedom: the feeling state in which we feel no internal or external constraints and/or limitations or restrictions and/or necessities.

And in turn, to be authentic, we must exist in a state of relaxedness.

It is in this state of relaxedness, where we can breathe freely and vibrate as liberated life energy, that our sensing and feeling ability is most infallible.

Relaxational intelligence and the ability to sense and feel allow us both the disclosure and revelation of our personal beingness and suchness and the most intelligent perception of all reality.

Because feeling is the first and most fundamental and all-other-skills-penetrating ability to experience everything.

Experiencing without feeling is not possible. And life without experiencing does (actually) not exist.

The relaxed and (in this sense) free state enables truly real and complete feeling and equips it at the same time with the highest possible organismic intelligence.

Thus, we are always in the most intelligent and alive state when we are relaxed and thus energetically free.

As long as we remain in this relaxed state and act

contentment: the state and feeling of nourishment, tranquility, wholeness and freedom.

organize: to bring a system into such a favorable coherent arrangement that this system has a fluid function-ality or all the characteristics of a healthy living organism, so that a cer-tain purpose is fulfilled or a certain goal is achieved.

emotional intelligence: the experien-tial knowledge of the meaning of one's own emotions and of how to deal or/ and be with them appropriately.

with it, and are not torn out of it, we are in and experience the feeling state of freedom. At any such moment or period of time.

However, apart from such moments or periods or phases, the more the basic satisfaction and contentment in the totality of our life has grown real, infallible and stable, the more we enlarge, widen and deepen the feeling state of being free as the basic existential state of our life.

Basic satisfaction and contentment and the state of being free, as guarantees of quality of life, are possible through higher life mastery and through more deeply internalized life skills mastery.

IV.

The Most Important

Life Skills

Contentment And Freedom

Learning And Organizational Intelligence

Action Intelligence And Self-Sufficiency

Rationality And Pragmatism

Groundedness And Realism

Communicational And Language Intelligence

General And Behavioral Intelligence

Motivational And Emotional Intelligence

Relaxational And Attentional Intelligence

Feeling Intelligence And Authenticity

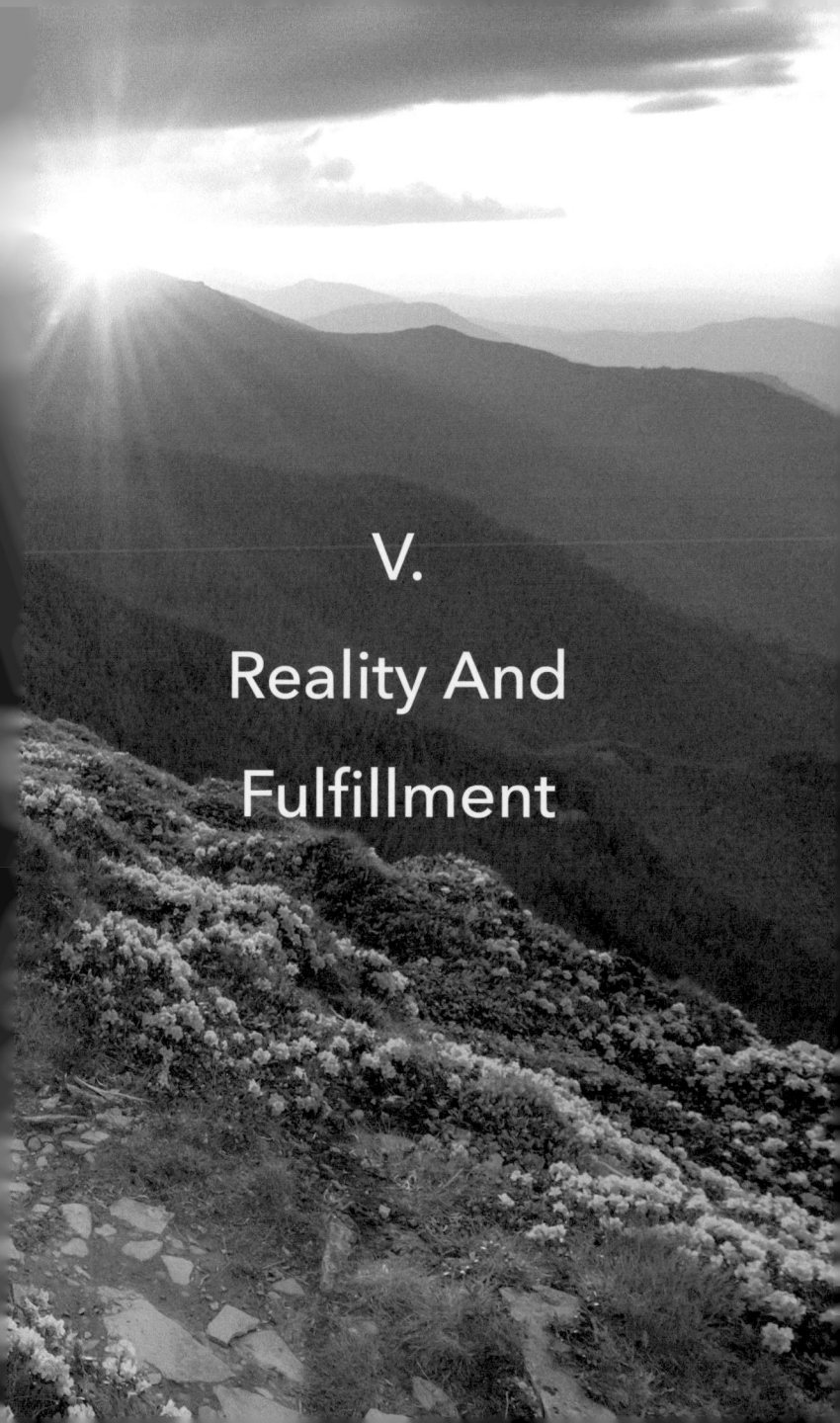

V.

Reality And

Fulfillment

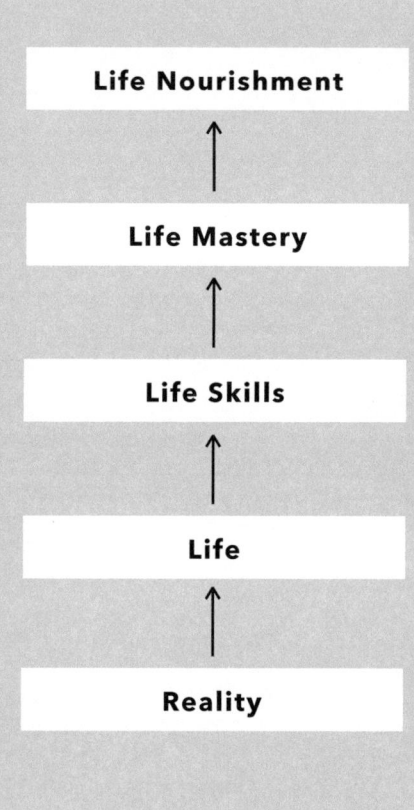

If our heart is full, if we enjoy the best of health and vibrant vitality, and if our life is permeated with contentment and freedom, then all this is not only beautiful, but also a sign that we have also had good fortune in our life so far; or favorable circumstances.

When or through what do we have good luck or favorable circumstances?

Favorable circumstances depend on how we come into the world, with which predispositions therefore, where in the world we are born, in which family or with which people, in which society, in which culture and, last but not least, also in which local and overall world situation we live.

In both possible cases, thus in the case of a life under more favorable circumstances as well as in the case of a life under more difficult circumstances, substantial life knowledge is crucial and decisive.

And perhaps, if not quite certainly, such life knowledge is more necessary and valuable precisely in more difficult or not so favorable circumstances.

We arrive at substantial life knowledge through experience and development, which occur when we open ourselves to life in a perceptive and feeling way.

With this life knowledge, we achieve the valuable goal of contentment and freedom, both a state in which we can exist and both also life skills consisting of the knowledge that makes that state possible.

All twenty basic and most important life skills, which represent both a state and the corresponding knowledge and skills, and which we can sufficiently recognize, practice, internalize, and use to achieve life mastery and thereby a fulfilling life, are:

Relaxational Intelligence, Feeling Intelligence and Authenticity.

Attentional Intelligence, Motivational Intelligence and Emotional Intelligence.

General Intelligence and Behavioral Intelligence.

Communicational Intelligence and Language Intelligence.

Groundedness and Realism.

Rationality and Pragmatism.

Action Intelligence and Self-Sufficiency.

Learning Intelligence and Organizational Intelligence.

Contentment and Freedom.

We experience and understand the value and importance of these life skills through life itself.

Within the big whole, that is called reality-and-its-laws, and equipped with the possibilities of being human or having homo-sapiens-membership, we have to or can face our adulthood thoughtfully, consciously and clearly, because not only practice makes perfect, but (even before that) also the courage to experience.

All twenty life skills are not something we can choose, nor something we can decide against. They come automatically by being alive. Moreover, there is also no watertight reason for not accepting them. The life skills are, after all, the skills of *life*. And they are also the skills *for* life at the same time. For this reason, they are always our best investment for the future and our best equipment for the everlasting present.

For our adulthood and for mastering our life, we should have sufficiently understood and internalized the life skills, indeed, preferably almost or completely mastered them.

Then we have the power to bring about a more fulfilling or a completely fulfilled life. We fully possess the human prerequisites for this.

The importance of life skills is obvious. However, this also means that all processes that largely determine our lives, such as upbringing, education, training and, yes, the nature of the prevailing social structure and also culture, should be (transformed) in such a way that the natural development and mastery of the truly necessary life skills is made possible or even guaranteed.

Because then we master the necessities of life.

Then we can also realize beyond what is necessary some, several or numerous such possibilities that make life possibly, additionally or truly more valuable. Then we can go up to the highest dimensions of realization:

To the dimension of creativity. To the dimension of intellectual nourishment. To the dimension of personal self-realization. To the dimension of nurturing togetherness. To the dimension of most nourishing well-being. To the dimension of deepest or purest spirituality or way of existence.

Everything is open and everything is possible. Especially if we are strongly rooted in all life skills, and of course, if fate is reasonably or even distinctly kind to us.

Further Publications

By Ioannis Tzivanakis

IOANNIS TZIVANAKIS

LEXICON OF LIFE

ITV

life
mastery
decoded

IOANNIS **TZIVANAKIS**

Ioannis Tzivanakis

Attention
Counseling

ITV

ADHD
DECODED

IOANNIS TZIVANAKIS

THE SOURCES OF ADHD & THEIR
TRANSFORMATIVE POWER

ITV

Publisher: Ioannis Tzivanakis Verlag, Hamburg 2022.

Printed in Germany.

ISBN 978-3-940493-37-8

www.lifeskillsmastery.net

Bibliographic information published by the Deutsche
Nationalbibliothek (German National Library): The Deutsche
Nationalbibliothek lists this publication in the Deutsche
Nationalbibliografie (German National Bibliography).

Quote on page 22 from: Erich Fromm: Die Furcht vor
der Freiheit (The Fear Of Freedom), Munich 2008, page 11.

About The Author

Ioannis Tzivanakis studied
linguistics and philosophy of
language at the University of
Bremen. His main focus was
semantics, consciousness re-
search and holism.

Since 1996 he works as a trainer, coach and consultant in
the areas of *Life Mastery*, *Life Skills*, *Spirituality*, *Learning Intelligence* and *ADHD* both in Germany and worldwide.

In 2006 and 2007 he published four issues of the Learning Intelligence Magazine on the topics of *learning foun-
dations*, *learning intelligence*, *management* and *spirituality*.

His already published books are "ADHD Decoded" (2018),
"Lexicon Of Life" (2021) and "Life Mastery Decoded" (2022).

More information on his programs, courses, seminars and
coaching areas can be found at:

www.tzivanakis.com